W9-AMB-178

WITHDRAWN
WELLESLEY FREE LIBRARY

WELLESLEY FREE LIBRARY
WELLESLEY, MASS. 02482

HOW TO DEAL

DOING THE RIGHT THING

LINDEN MCNEILLY

Rourke
Educational Media

A Division of
Carson
Dellosa
Education

rourkeeducationalmedia.com

ROURKE'S
SCHOOL to HOME
CONNECTIONS
BEFORE AND DURING READING ACTIVITIES

Before Reading: *Building Background Knowledge and Vocabulary*

Building background knowledge can help children process new information and build upon what they already know. Before reading a book, it is important to tap into what children already know about the topic. This will help them develop their vocabulary and increase their reading comprehension.

Questions and Activities to Build Background Knowledge:

1. Look at the front cover of the book and read the title. What do you think this book will be about?
2. What do you already know about this topic?
3. Take a book walk and skim the pages. Look at the table of contents, photographs, captions, and bold words. Did these text features give you any information or predictions about what you will read in this book?

Vocabulary: *Vocabulary Is Key to Reading Comprehension*

Use the following directions to prompt a conversation about each word.

- Read the vocabulary words.
- What comes to mind when you see each word?
- What do you think each word means?

> ### Vocabulary Words:
> - accomplishments
> - alternative
> - bystanders
> - dilemma
> - ethics
> - influence
> - isolates
> - neglect
> - property
> - racism
> - revenge
> - suspects

During Reading: *Reading for Meaning and Understanding*

To achieve deep comprehension of a book, children are encouraged to use close reading strategies. During reading, it is important to have children stop and make connections. These connections result in deeper analysis and understanding of a book.

 Close Reading a Text

During reading, have children stop and talk about the following:

- Any confusing parts
- Any unknown words
- Text to text, text to self, text to world connections
- The main idea in each chapter or heading

Encourage children to use context clues to determine the meaning of any unknown words. These strategies will help children learn to analyze the text more thoroughly as they read.

When you are finished reading this book, turn to page 46 for **Text-Dependent Questions** and an **Extension Activity**.

TABLE OF CONTENTS

Decisions, Decisions.................................4

How to Spot a Bully 12

Take Action on Abuse 18

Dilemmas Are Double Trouble 24

Pressure From Peers 30

Slow Down the Anger Train 36

Activity..44

Glossary...45

Index 46

Text-Dependent Questions........................46

Extension Activity 46

Bibliography..47

About the Author...................................48

CHAPTER 1

DECISIONS, DECISIONS

inn walks home after school with a large group of classmates. Some of the kids he walks with stop at a busy market to buy snacks. He sees one of them, Matt, steal candy bars. When Matt gets outside, he says, "Here, dude, I got you something." Matt shoves a candy bar into Finn's hands. Finn is hungry just looking at it. He stands there holding the candy bar, wondering what to do. He feels sort of sick knowing that it's stolen, but no one else seems to care. "What are you waiting for?" says Matt as he hands out candy to others.

You are faced with decisions every day. Some are routine, like choosing which shoes to wear or when to do your homework. Other decisions involve more thinking. Like Finn, a friend might pressure you to make a decision you aren't comfortable with. You might be tempted to do the wrong thing, like taking **property** that isn't yours.

You might have to choose between two things you want equally. Your choice might make someone angry, or make you feel unpopular. Doing the right thing can take courage. Good decision-making requires you to know who you are and what you value. It isn't always easy.

The best choice isn't always obvious. Your friends and feelings can steer you the wrong way. But you can establish a basis for choosing the right thing. Good decisions follow your **ethics** and morals. They are based on your family's values. They are safe and legal. But how do you know what's right every time?

Choices Make Your Brain Better

Did you know that your choices help shape the way your brain develops in adolescence? The neural connections you use frequently strengthen, while those you use less are cut away through a process called synaptic pruning. Thinking carefully and choosing wisely actually trains your brain to keep doing that throughout your life.

Feelings can often give you a signal. In the situation you read about, Finn felt bad taking the candy. Paying attention to your own feelings, despite what others around you are doing, can help you make good decisions.

Sometimes, friends who break rules want you to break them too. If you join in on your friend's bad decision, it can make your friend feel less guilty. He or she might think that your participation makes the behavior more okay. In the story you read, sharing the stolen candy helps Matt feel generous instead of guilty. But this does not change the rules. Stealing is always wrong and against the law. It's also illegal to take things that you know are stolen.

Anyone involved with stealing or other rule-breaking or illegal acts is eventually going to have trouble with adults in charge, including parents, teachers, or law enforcement officers. If friends pressure you to do something against the rules, you need to tell them you're not interested. You should also hang out with different people who make good decisions.

CHAPTER 2

HOW TO SPOT A BULLY

very day, Kasim dreads getting on the bus. Nam, a kid he hardly knows, seeks Kasim out. He purposely pushes Kasim and steps on his feet. "When are you going back home to Iran?" Nam asks. "I was born here, I'm American," Kasim says, but Nam keeps abusing him. Lara and Melanie are usually nearby. In class, the girls are nice to Kasim. But on the bus, they laugh along with Nam as he insults Kasim. Kasim tries to catch their eyes to get help, but they look away from him. The bus driver never seems to notice.

Nam is a prejudicial bully. He insults and hurts people who are different from him. Like most bullies, Nam likes to have an audience. Bullies use social power to be cruel to others and get attention. This makes them feel important.

Lara and Melanie are guilty **bystanders** because they help keep the bullying going by laughing. If you witness bullying, you should never laugh, agree with, or otherwise egg the bully on. Bullies depend on bystanders for approval.

The Cruelty of Prejudice

In prejudicial bullying, a bully picks on someone because of his or her culture, race, gender, or sexual identity. The bully assumes or makes up negative things and uses them to insult victims in front of others. Prejudice is at the core of hate crimes, which are against the law.

Most bystanders to bullying have the power to stop it. If you witness bullying, take a deep breath and gather your courage. Then, use a firm voice to say, "Cut it out," "That's not funny," "You're being a racist," or something similar. Let the victim know you support him or her and won't tolerate the bullying. You can also help by asking others to join you in calling out the bully's **racism** and cruelty.

Bystanders Bust Bullying

Because bullies want popularity, they need their peers' admiration. If bystanders do not give positive attention, or when they try to stop the bullying, bullies often lose interest. Telling bullies that they are wrong or mean is a very powerful thing for bystanders to do.

If you are the victim of bullying, first stand up for yourself. Call out the bully's bad behavior in a strong voice. Then, ask others around you to help. Report bullying to a trusted adult as soon as possible. It takes courage to confront a bully, but it helps you and others in your community. Everyone deserves to feel safe and respected. No one deserves to be hassled for riding the bus, being at school, or just going about their day.

CHAPTER

3

TAKE ACTION
ON ABUSE

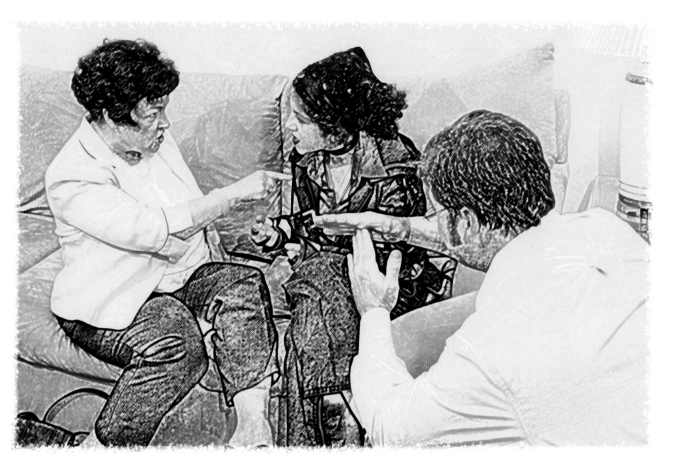

assah and Tai have been school friends for years. They eat lunch together every school day and talk in the hallway. "Can you come over this weekend?" Yassah often asks. "No, I'm busy," Tai always replies. She never visits Yassah at home or invites Yassah to her home. Sometimes, Yassah notices that Tai has bruises or burns on her arms. "What happened?" she asks. "Oh, I just had this accident, I'm so clumsy," Tai says. Yassah **suspects** that someone at home is hurting Tai.

Child abuse is cruel treatment of a young person done by a family member or caregiver regularly or repeatedly. It can include physical abuse, emotional abuse, sexual abuse, or **neglect**. Different laws define abuse from state to state.

It's Hard to Tell the Truth

Reporting abuse can be extremely hard emotionally, especially for the victim, because children can be attached to and dependent on their abusers. Abusers can be loving and kind sometimes but abusive at other times. It can be confusing to the victim, who simply wishes for the abuse to stop.

Child abuse victims might be told to keep the abuse a secret. They may be threatened that bad things will happen if they tell the truth. This is one of the ways that abusers get away with bad behavior. For these reasons and more, victims often feel ashamed. They need to know that they have done nothing wrong. If you have been abused, it's not your fault. You deserve better.

Victims of child abuse often hope that things will improve on their own. "Shame **isolates** a young person by keeping him or her quiet about what is actually happening," says psychologist Dr. Carl Pickhardt. But staying silent won't bring change.

It takes courage to stop abuse. If you are being abused, you can help stop the pain by bringing the situation into the open as soon as possible. Talk to a trusted adult such as a relative, teacher, counselor, principal, doctor, or police officer. If you know someone who you think might be experiencing abuse, share the information right away. Tell an adult who you trust and respect. Ending abuse can help begin healing for everyone.

The Law About Reporting Abuse

Certain professional adults, by law, must report suspected child abuse. They are called mandated reporters. *Though the list is different from state to state, it can include social workers, teachers, health care workers, childcare providers, law enforcement officers, mental health professionals, and other educators and medical professionals.*

CHAPTER 4

DILEMMAS ARE DOUBLE TROUBLE

Stay? Go?

arco has been looking forward to his scout camping trip for months. The troop has been raising money, and Marco plans to earn several badges while he is at camp. At the last minute, Marco's parents tell him that his cousins are going to be in town for a visit. "We want you to stay home," his father tells him. "You rarely get to see your cousins. Do the camping trip next year." Marco is torn. He wants to spend time with his cousins, but he has been planning the camping trip for a long time. He doesn't want to let his troop down. He doesn't want to let his family down either.

You may have experienced a **dilemma**, or a situation in which both choices have good and bad outcomes. Marco will miss the camping trip if he stays home with his cousins. But if he goes camping, he'll miss a rare visit with his cousins. With dilemmas, there's no clear best choice.

What's the Big Idea?

It's important to think of the big picture when you make decisions. Who does this affect besides you? What does your greater community think, and how will they view you later after you make this decision? When faced with disappointment, what can you do to get over that and move forward?

Making a list of pros and cons can shed light on what to do in a dilemma. Giving a value to each item helps you compare your choices. Organize the list with the top values next to each other. This can help you see what's most important.

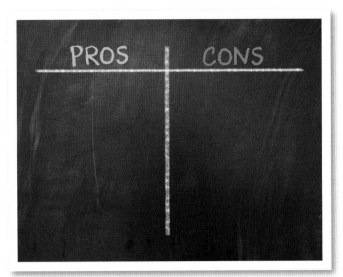

Sometimes, it helps to look at the long-term and short-term results of a decision. In the dilemma you read about, Marco might consider that his troop may plan more camping trips. But he might not see his cousins again for a long time. He should ask himself: Which decision will have a longer lasting effect?

Another way to handle dilemmas is to find **alternative** solutions. If you are torn between two things, can you find a way to do both things, but differently? For example, Marco might be able to plan a separate trip to visit his cousins. Exploring alternatives gives you more choices.

Give a Little, Get a Little

Sometimes dilemmas can be solved through compromise, which is giving up a little on each side. Could Marco go camping with his troop and leave early to have time with his cousins? Could his cousins attend the camping trip with him? Think outside the box when deciding what to do about dilemmas.

CHAPTER

5

PRESSURE FROM PEERS

**P**edro loves to ride his BMX bike. He rides on dirt trails and likes to jump and do tricks. He practices every day and pushes himself to try new things. He wants to get better so he can compete in a year or two. His older

neighbor, David, races and has a cool bike. David says, "Come ride on the train trestle. It's easy." Pedro knows that the trestle is high, narrow, and very dangerous. He says, "No, I don't think so." But David says, "Are you afraid? You can't be chicken if you're going to win someday." Pedro wants to prove he's as brave as David.

Doing something to prove that you're not afraid often means trouble. Peer pressure is a major reason why young people sometimes make poor decisions, according to researcher Dr. Gina Tomé. When peers try to embarrass you or tease you, the pressure is on.

Psychology and criminology expert Dr. James McCue explains that peer pressure can create a "hot" situation. Change the subject, do something else, or simply don't act. When your feelings aren't ruling you, the situation becomes "cold." Then you can make better decisions.

Peers Pile on Pressure

*Scientific studies of pre-teen and teen brains show that peers have a strong **influence** on decisions. Teens step outside their comfort zones more with peers. This is both positive and negative. Peers with good standards can influence good choices. But peers who like danger might influence you negatively. Pay attention to peer pressure.*

If a friend pressures you, ask yourself why. Sometimes it makes others feel powerful to convince you to take risks. Consider that friends might be lying to you, exaggerating their own experiences, or trying to get you to take the blame for something. Real friends do not put others into unsafe situations.

Great Ways to Say No

When you've decided not to do something that makes you uncomfortable, you don't have to explain yourself. You want to sound strong and in control. Some good phrases to use include: "Sorry, I can't today," "That doesn't look like fun," "Not my thing," and "Got to go now."

It helps to practice refusal phrases at home. Then you'll know what to say when others try to influence you. You will feel less nervous and on the spot if you are ready to calmly say no. Remember that anyone who tries to embarrass you into doing something isn't thinking of you at all.

arah likes school pretty well, but she's not a top student like her sister Trina. Math is difficult for Sarah but very easy for Trina, who competes on the math scholars team. Trina brags about her good grades in math and makes fun of Sarah for having a hard time. "Look what I got," Trina says as she puts her A+ test on the refrigerator. Sarah crumples her own B- math test into a ball and runs to her room. She's so mad she wants to rip Trina's test off the refrigerator.

Sarah's shame and anger are real. Her sister is being unkind and showing off. If you've been in a situation like this, you know that strong feelings can be very powerful. But acting on them in the heat of the moment means the feelings are in control and you are not.

Take a minute to do nothing. Breathing, sitting quietly, or simply getting away from the situation gives you control over your feelings. Later, think of a better solution than getting **revenge**. Feelings change quickly, but actions, especially in a family or among friends, can cause lasting damage.

HALT Those Feelings!

When emotions run high, use the HALT method of checking what's going on before you act. HALT stands for Hungry, Angry, Lonely, or Tired. If you are experiencing any of these feelings, you might have trouble making good decisions, according to Signe Whitson, an author and expert on bullying and crisis intervention. Eat something, cool down, talk to a friend, or get some rest before doing anything extreme.

When someone repeatedly hurts your feelings, you need to tell them to stop. Sometimes people close to you don't realize how much little comments or actions hurt. Telling them firmly and asking for them to change their behavior can make things better.

Siblings and friends often struggle with competition. Sometimes show-offs, like Trina in the story you read, are hiding problems of their own. If you find yourself competing with someone, remind yourself that everyone has strengths and weaknesses. Someone else's **accomplishments** are not yours, just as yours are not theirs.

Super Sad? There's Help

Sometimes, you might feel alone and think that everyone is against you. You might experience low moods, which can lead to thoughts of self-harm or suicide. Always tell someone if you feel like harming yourself. Tell a trusted adult such as a parent, relative, teacher, clergy member, or medical professional who can help you get the support you need. The National Suicide Prevention Lifeline is available 24 hours a day to provide help at 1-800-273-8255.

Doing the right thing isn't always easy. You might have to go against the crowd when everyone else is having fun. You might have to do something that makes someone angry. You might have to use courage to face a bully or an abuser. You might feel shame or embarrassment.

The choices you make and the actions you take can be powerful. Bystanders really can shut bullying down. Telling difficult truths can bring needed changes. You can help others and improve your own life. Your decisions can help shape your life now and in the future.

WHAT'S RIGHT?: THE GAME

Make a board game to help you and your friends think through situations and practice making good decisions. Decide how many players will play your game. Game play should include situation cards, a game board, a token for each player, and other pieces such as dice, spinners, or timers.

Cut paper into 20 or more situation cards. On each, write a situation in which a young person has an important decision to make. Include examples of bullying, peer pressure, angry feelings, dilemmas, and more. Use poster board to make your game board. Sketch it in pencil first. Then use markers or colored pencils to fill it in. Practice playing the game so you can explain the rules.

Play the game with your friends! Make sure to read the cards aloud and discuss how to make a good decision in each situation.

GLOSSARY

accomplishments (uh-KAHM-plish-ments): things done or completed successfully

alternative (awl-TUR-nuh-tiv): different from the usual way of doing things

bystanders (BYE-stan-durs): people who are at a place where something happens to someone else; spectators

dilemma (duh-LEM-uh): a situation in which any possible choice has some disadvantages

ethics (ETH-iks): personal beliefs about right and wrong

influence (IN-floo-uhns): to have an effect on someone or something

isolates (EYE-suh-lates): separates from other people

neglect (ni-GLEKT): the failure to take care of or pay attention to something or someone

property (PRAH-pur-tee): anything owned by an individual

racism (RAY-siz-uhm): the belief that a particular race is better than others; treating others unfairly or cruelly because of their race

revenge (ri-VENJ): something you do to get back at someone for causing injury or harm

suspects (suh-SPEKTS): thinks that something may be true; guesses or supposes

INDEX

abuse(r) 20, 21, 22, 23, 42

bully(ing) 12, 14, 15, 16, 17, 39,
    42, 43

competition 41

courage 7, 16, 17, 23, 42

decision(s) 6, 8, 9, 10, 11, 26, 28, 32,
    33, 39, 43

feeling(s) 8, 9, 33, 38, 39, 40

friend(s) 6, 8, 10, 11, 19, 34, 39, 41

illegal 10, 11

long-term 28

peer pressure 32, 33

prejudicial bullying 15

self-harm 41

TEXT-DEPENDENT QUESTIONS

1. What is a prejudicial bully?
2. How can bystanders change bullying?
3. Why is peer pressure so hard to resist?
4. Why do some victims of child abuse want to keep quiet?
5. Why is it useful to practice ways to say no?

EXTENSION ACTIVITY

Think about a recent time you or someone you know had a dilemma. Make a list of the pros and cons of each side of the dilemma. Then, give each pro or con a number value to rank how important it is. If you compare numbers in all the columns, does it help you decide the right thing to do? If not, what could you change about the list and the values? Make the change and try to find the best decision.

BIBLIOGRAPHY

"About Good Decision-Making." Kids Matter: Australian Primary Schools Mental Health Initiative. https://www.kidsmatter.edu.au/families/about-behaviour/making-decisions/learning-make-good-decisions-and-solve-problems. (accessed November 1, 2018).

Decety, Jean, and Jason M. Cowell. "Our Brains Are Wired for Morality: Evolution, Development, and Neuroscience." Frontiers for Young Minds (March 9, 2016): https://kids.frontiersin.org/article/10.3389/frym.2016.00003. (accessed November 25, 2018).

Kidder, Rushworth M. *Good Kids, Tough Choices: How Parents Can Help Their Children Do the Right Thing*. Hoboken, NJ: Jossey-Bass, 2010.

Lyness, D'Arcy. "Dealing with Peer Pressure." Kids' Health from Nemours (July 2015): https://kidshealth.org/en/kids/peer-pressure.html. (accessed November 8, 2018).

McCue, James. "A Parent's Guide to Why Teens Make Bad Decisions." The Conversation (Jan 2018): https://theconversation.com/a-parents-guide-to-why-teens-make-bad-decisions-88246. (accessed November 1, 2018).

Monteverde, Matt. *Making Smart Choices About Violence, Gangs, and Bullying*. New York: Rosen Central, 2008.

Pickhardt, Carl. *Why Good Kids Act Cruel*. Naperville, IL: Sourcebooks, 2010.

Tomé, Gina, et al. "How Can Peer Group Influence the Behavior of Adolescents: Explanatory Model." *Global Journal of Health Science* (March 2012): https://www.ncbi.nlm.nih.gov/pmc/articles/PMC4777050/. (accessed November 3, 2018).

Wang, Jing, et al. "School Bullying Among Adolescents in the United States: Physical, Verbal, Relational, and Cyber." *Journal of Adolescent Health* 45, no. 4 (October 2009): 368–375, https://www.ncbi.nlm.nih.gov/pmc/articles/PMC2751860/pdf/nihms-110973.pdf. (accessed November 22, 2018).

Whitson, Signe. *8 Keys to End Bullying*. New York: W. W. Norton & Company, 2014.

ABOuT THE AuTHOR

Linden McNeilly has written numerous books for young readers. She taught school for many years and now spends her time researching crazy facts about insects, flowers, and history, painting birds, and enjoying the outdoors with her family on the Central Coast of California.

© 2020 Rourke Educational Media

All rights reserved. No part of this book may be reproduced or utilized in any form or by any means, electronic or mechanical including photocopying, recording, or by any information storage and retrieval system without permission in writing from the publisher.

www.rourkeeducationalmedia.com

PHOTO CREDITS: Cover photos (Top) Luis Molinero | Shutterstock.com, (Bottom) Africa Studio | Shutterstock.com; Page 4-5: istock.com | Wavebreakmedia; Page 6-7: istock.com |seb_ra, istock.com | tepic, istock.com | Mikhail Spaskov; Page 8-9: istock.com | mandygodbehear, shutterstock.com | Andrey_Popov; Page 10-11: istock.com | WTolenaars, istock.com | yacobchuk, istock.com | Wavebreakmedia; Page 12-13: istock.com | burakkarademir/Marina113; Page 14-15: istock.com | Motortion, shutterstock.com | Africa Studio; Page 16-17: istock.com | omgimages, istock.com | igor_kell, istock.com | monkeybusinessimages; Page 18-19: istock.com | lisafx; Page 20-21: istock.com | Feverpitched, istock.com | ejwhite; Page 22-23: istock.com | tommaso79, istock.com | Povozniuk; Page 24-25: istock.com | PredragImages; Page 26-27: istock.com | PredragImages/searagen; Page 28-29: istock.com | Chainarong Prasertthai, istock.com | AndreyPopov; Page 30-31: istock.com | Surf-Skate-Ski; Page 32-33: shutterstock.com | anuskiserrano, shutterstock.com | y Sweet Memento Photography, shutterstock.com | Pixel-Shot; Page 34-35: istock.com | Willowpix, shutterstock.com | Sabphoto, 99117117 ©Picturemakersllc | Dreamstime.com; Page 36-37: istock.com | imtmphoto; Page 38-39: istock.com | qingwa, istock.com | Bojan89; Page 40-41: istock.com | AntonioGuillem, shutterstock.com | CREATISTA; Page 42-43: istock.com | igor_kell, Editorial-shutterserstock.com | Cassiohabib.

Edited by: Kim Thompson

Produced by Blue Door Education for Rourke Educational Media. Cover and interior design by: Jennifer Dydyk

Library of Congress PCN Data

Doing the Right Thing / Linden McNeilly
(How To Deal)
ISBN 978-1-73161-491-9 (hard cover)
ISBN 978-1-73161-298-4 (soft cover)
ISBN 978-1-73161-596-1 (e-Book)
ISBN 978-1-73161-701-9 (e-Pub)
Library of Congress Control Number: 2019932326

Rourke Educational Media
Printed in the United States of America,
North Mankato, Minnesota